EIGHT NIGHTS, EIGHT LIGHTS

Family Values for Each Night of Hanukkah

by Rabbi Kerry M. Olitzky

ALEF DESIGN GROUP

Library of Congress Cataloging-in-Publication Data

Olitzky, Kerry M.
    Eight nights, eight lights : family values for each night of Hanukkah / by Kerry M. Olitzky.
        p.   cm.
    ISBN 1-881283-09-7 : $8.95
    1. Hanukkah. 2. Jewish families—Religious life.   I. Title.
    BM695.H3043   1994
    296.4'35—dc20   94-3619
                                                    CIP

ISBN # 0-831283-08-9

Published by Alef Design Group

Alef Design Group

4423 Fruitland Avenue

Los Angeles, California 90058

(213) 582-1200

TABLE OF CONTENTS

PREFACE

There are eight lights in the Hanukkah menorah. Known as a *hanukkiyah*, this menorah, this candle holder is only used for Hanukkah. In addition, in order to prevent us from making use of the light for purposes other than shining their unpretentious splendor on our celebration of Hanukkah, there is an extra candle, the *shammash* or helper candle. We extend the light of this candle in order to light the others. As we have learned, by extending light in the world, we can add to it while not diminishing our own.

There are those who have suggested that the spheres of the tree of life which come to us through the Jewish mystical tradition of kabbalah may be used to identify themes of light for each night of Hanukkah. While I have used these mystical spheres to guide me in the selection of themes for the lighting of candles each night, I am mindful of Rabbi Hillel's advice to "go out and see what the people are doing." Therefore, I have selected themes which reflect the nature of contemporary Jewish life and the celebration of Hanukkah in our midst, trying to infuse the secular with the sacred.

In a period of eight days, Hanukkah offers us a glimpse of the divine, an opportunity to rededicate ourselves to all that is holy in the world. May the lights of Hanukkah illumine your path in the world as you make your life's journey through it.

What Really Happened: The Story of Hanukkah

anukkah (also spelled *Chanukah* and *Hanukah* and probably ten other ways) means "rededication"—and is related to the Hebrew word for "education." It is celebrated in the winter on Kislev 25 (near the time of the winter solstice, the darkest day of the year when we yearn for light)—generally in December. Hanukkah refers to the eight-day rededication of the ancient Temple in Jerusalem which had been defiled by the Assyrian-Greeks in an attempt to totally Hellenize Jerusalem and Israel. The "Festival of Lights," as it is sometimes called, is observed for eight days throughout the Jewish world in celebration of this miraculous victory of the spirit.

When the rabbis sensed that the military victory of the Maccabees was taking precedent in the minds of the Jewish people, it was they who reminded the people of the true miracle through the introduction of the story of the miracle cruse of oil. According to tradition, the oil burned for eight days. Whether it burned that long or not, as I see it, the miraculous victory was so great it seemed as if the Temple menorah glowed throughout the eight day festival of rededication.

But how did all this happen in the first place?

7

It seems that Alexander the Great of Greece had conquered Israel and most of the world by the year 334 B.C.E. (Before the Common Era). When he died in 323 B.C.E., his empire was divided. Israel which was (and still is) located between Syria and Greece was valuable to both parts of the divided empire and became a political pawn (and battlefield), sometimes ruled by Syria and other times by Egypt.

In 175 B.C.E. when Israel came under Syrian control, Antiochus IV (Antiochus Epiphanes) became king of Syria. Since he was afraid of losing Israel as had his predecessors so often, he sought ways to strengthen his empire. Therefore, he decreed that all of his subjects must worship the same (Greek) gods and follow the same (Greek) customs. As a result, the Jews were not permitted to study Torah, keep Shabbat, or do anything Jewish.

Some Jews, called Hellenists, liked the Greek way of life. They wore Greek clothing and spoke the Greek language. Others, their opponents, called the *Hasidim* (not to be confused with modern *Hasidim* known by their black coats, fur hats and *payot*), did not approve of Hellenization of any kind. They felt that the influence of Greek culture on Judaism would eventually destroy it. The *Hasidim* began their opposition with a simple refusal to obey the laws of Antiochus. As a result, they suffered harshly. Thus, there was no choice for them but to rebel. In a sense, therefore, Israel was embroiled in a civil war.

Beginning in the small town of Modi'in, not far from Jerusalem, a priest named Mattathias started the revolt. He called on others to join him: "Whoever is for God (come) with me." The small band of Mattathias and his five sons began a guerrilla-type offensive in the hills against the mighty Assyrian-Greek armies. Later, in the year 165 B.C.E. led by one of the sons, called

Judah ha-Maccabee (Judah the Hammer—apparently because of the mighty blows he struck), this small army called the Maccabees forced the foreign army from Jerusalem. This indeed was a miraculous victory. And on the 25th day of Kislev of that year, they rededicated the Temple which had been defiled. They cleansed it, removed the statues of Zeus and other Greek gods. Following the model of Sukkot which they had not been able to celebrate, this Biblically-proscribed dedication of the Temple lasted for eight days. Slowly, the aspects of the Sukkot celebration in the context of Hanukkah gave way to particular events reserved for Hanukkah only.

Transforming Candles into Holy Light

he notion of *pirsumat hanes* (literally, "to make known the miracle") is the prism through which we view the entire celebration of Hanukkah. That's one of the reasons the *hanukkiyah* is lit in a place where the family gathers—so that all may bear witness to the miracle of its light. Invite people to light candles with you, especially those who may not previously have had the opportunity, whether they are newcomers to Judaism, to the community, or finding their way home to Judaism.

Remember that the candles are not holy themselves. Rather, as we have been taught by Rabbi Shmuel in the Babylonian Talmud (Shabbat 22a), they are merely instruments of holiness. What we do with their light, in a metaphysical sense, is totally up to us.

1. Place your Hanukkah menorah (hanukkiyah) in your window so that everyone can see its light. It's a way to share the miracle with the world. Traditional Jews believe that all of the candles in the hanukkiyah should be on one level—with the shammash separate or higher—so that you can distinguish one light from the other. Often modern hanukkiyot have candles which are on different levels.

2. Load your candles in your hanukkiyah from the right, one for each night. (If your hanukkiyah is made for oil, fill it up with olive oil and use wicks.) So on the first night, you should have one candle (plus the shammash), on the second night, two (plus the shammash) and so on. Some people use a new shammash each night. Others use the same shammash throughout the festival, blowing it out each night after it has finished its job—until the last night when you let the shammash burn down completely.

3. After you have said the Hanukkah blessings, light the shammash. After you have lit the shammash, you may light the candles in the hanukkiyah. Light from the left, beginning with the candle designated for the particular night you are celebrating. On the first night, you light only one candle. On the second night, you first light the candle designated for that second night, then the first. On the third night, you first light the candle for the third night, then continue in descending order to the candle for the second night, then the first and so on throughout the eight days. This approach to candle-lighting, according to Rabbi Hillel, allows us to increase light in the world—especially in such a time of darkness. It is the custom of one particular community to add a hanukkiyah each night; that practice really increases the light!

On Lighting the Ḥanukkiyah

(on each night)

בָּרוּךְ אַתָּה, יהוה אֱלֹהֵינוּ, מֶלֶךְ הָעוֹלָם, אֲשֶׁר קִדְּשָׁנוּ בְּמִצְוֹתָיו וְצִוָּנוּ לְהַדְלִיק נֵר שֶׁל חֲנֻכָּה.

Praised are You, Adonai our God, Sovereign of the world who has made us holy with *mitzvot* and instructed us to light the Ḥanukkah lights.

(on each night)

בָּרוּךְ אַתָּה, יהוה אֱלֹהֵינוּ, מֶלֶךְ הָעוֹלָם, שֶׁעָשָׂה נִסִּים לַאֲבוֹתֵיהוּ בַּיָּמִים הָהֵם בַּזְּמָן הַזֶּה.

Praised are You, Adonai our God, Sovereign of the world who performed miracles for our ancestors at this season in ancient times.

(on first night only)

בָּרוּךְ אַתָּה, יהוה אֱלֹהֵינוּ, מֶלֶךְ הָעוֹלָם, שֶׁהֶחֱיָנוּ וְקִיְּמָנוּ וְהִגִּיעָנוּ לַזְּמָן הַזֶּה.

Praised are You, Adonai our God, Sovereign of the world who has given us life, sustained us, and helped us to reach this moment.

Following the lighting of the first candle, *Hanerot Hallalu* is recited:

הַנֵּרוֹת הַלָּלוּ אֲנַחְנוּ מַדְלִיקִין עַל הַנִּסִּים וְעַל הַנִּפְלָאוֹת,
וְעַל הַתְּשׁוּעוֹת וְעַל הַמִּלְחָמוֹת, שֶׁעָשִׂיתָ לַאֲבוֹתֵינוּ בַּיָּמִים
הָהֵם בַּזְּמַן הַזֶּה עַל יְדֵי כֹּהֲנֶיךָ הַקְּדוֹשִׁים. וְכָל-שְׁמוֹנַת יְמֵי
חֲנֻכָּה הַנֵּרוֹת הַלָּלוּ קֹדֶשׁ הֵם, וְאֵין לָנוּ רְשׁוּת לְהִשְׁתַּמֵּשׁ
בָּהֶם אֶלָּא לִרְאוֹתָם בִּלְבָד, כְּדֵי לְהוֹדוֹת וּלְהַלֵּל לִשְׁמְךָ
הַגָּדוֹל, עַל נִסֶּיךָ וְעַל נִפְלְאוֹתֶיךָ וְעַל יְשׁוּעָתֶךָ.

We kindle these lights (*hanerot hallalu*) [to remember] the miracles, the wonders, the salvations, and the battles which You performed for our ancestors in former days at this season through Your holy priest. During these eight days, these lights are sacred. We are not permitted to use them for mundane purposes, only to gaze at them [intently] as a way of thanking You for Your [unending] miracles, wonders, and salvations.

It's okay to work during Hanukkah. It's not one of those holidays which is Shabbat-like. But during the half-hour that the candles are burning (that's at least how long the candles should burn), put your work aside. Just enjoy the simple joy of bringing light into the world. And know deep in your soul that you had a part in it.

In some communities, it is traditional to light Hanukkah candles on the mornings of the festival as well—but without reciting the blessings. When you light candles during the day, people really know that the light has a special purpose. It also serves as a reminder for those who may have forgotten to light their *hanukkiyah* the night before. So light your candles during the day, as well. Remember: there is never enough Hanukkah light in the world.

Some Special Things to Remember

Remember to include the *Al Hanissim* section (a summary of the Hanukkah happening) during the Amidah section of your daily prayers and in Birkat ha-Mazon (Grace After Meals).

Don't forget to read the Hallel psalms (113-118) during the eight days. It helps us to remember that "Adonai is God who has given us light" (Psalm 118:27).

* * *

Reb Shelomo of Karlin, a hasidic rabbi, preferred wax candles for his menorah—which was really contrary to the rest of the community which preferred to use oil. He believed that wax candles left an impression on the wall where the menorah hung so that he could be reminded of the Hanukkah miracle all year long. The house which uses oil, he contended, bears no such mark.

One year he decided to take the advice of his colleagues and use oil in his Hanukkah menorah. The entire menorah caught on fire—nothing serious, just enough for the wall to be slightly scorched. But Reb Shelomo was pleased. "The oil menorah is soon forgotten," he taught, "but this time the mitzvah has left its mark on my home."

The First Night, The First Light
GEVURAH:
THE LIGHT OF COURAGE

Learning

udah and his brothers—and those who fought with them—had the kind of courage that it seems like we can only read about in history books. Perhaps that is what draws us to the Hanukkah festival each year. A small group of untrained men and presumably women entered into guerrilla-type warfare with the entire Assyrian-Greek army. Working in small ambush attack units, they succeeded in toppling a military giant. Through their persistence and determination, they regained control of the land of Israel. Their victory was incredible, even by the standards of modern warfare. Yet, it seems incomplete. There had to be more to their triumph than just a display of military prowess. That would seem to be insufficient to establish a festival in the middle of winter.

The rabbis agree. They wanted to steer the Jewish community clear of what was becoming a clear emphasis on the military victory of the Maccabees. Thus, the rabbis introduced the notion of "spiritual strength" into the celebration of Hanukkah. Listen to the well-known words of Zechariah (from the Haftarah for Shabbat Hanukkah) that they chose as their theme: "Not by might and not by power, but by My spirit, says Adonai"

(Zechariah 4:6). This is the kind of faith that the Maccabees also possessed. Perhaps it was this inner strength that really drove them to victory. They won because they believed that they could win. And then they acted on that belief.

We may think that Judah and the Maccabee's heroism is unparalleled—and it may be. But there is Maccabee strength in each one of us. We are all children of the Maccabees. As modern Jews, living with one foot each in both the Jewish and the secular world, the challenge we face is to retap that reservoir of courage that lies hidden deep inside the recesses of our souls. During Hanukkah, as we see ourselves reflected in the simple light of the candles burning, we are able to gather the courage to meet that challenge of modern Jewish life. The Maccabean legacy lives on, but only through us.

Doing

ecisions about what to do, especially to capture the spirit of the festival, are often difficult to make. The conversation usually begins, "So what do you want to do tonight?" Specific responses may vary, but they frequently sound like, "There's nothing to do." And often that's what happens. Nothing!

This year, we're not going to let that happen. Not tonight, not any of the eight nights of Hanukkah. Even while the candles are still burning in the *hanukkiyah*, let's try to understand the courage of the Maccabees and use it as a model for our own lives. But remember, lighting candles is not enough. We have to do more.

The Maccabean revolt was not spontaneous. It took some time to plan, and then time to carry out. Each step required courage. All decisions require courage. Of course, some courageous acts are unplanned: those you can never rehearse. They just demand of you to be all that you can be. No one can ask for more. Tonight, gather your family—around the kitchen table. It is usually the friendliest place in the house, where most important decisions are made. Even if it is just you and one other, remember, family is family, no matter who and how many live in your house. Invite your friends to join you, if you would like. You are about to make a decision that may change your life and the life of your family.

What is going on in your community, in your neighborhood, on your block—perhaps at school or at work—that calls to you to speak up? You realize that things need to be fixed, changed and yet you have remained silent. In the spirit of Hanukkah, with the model of Judah in front of you, you realize that it is time to take action. Discuss the challenge and possible solutions with one another around your table. Seize the decision. Make it your struggle, the one that drives your very being.

Usually we think of how little we can do in a world that is so full of daily challenges, so much in need of renewal. Yet, world repair is accomplished through the gathering of small sparks, one at a time, that together make a big light. Just as you place your *hanukkiyah* in the window so that others can behold the miracle of light, your action should take place where others can see it so that they can serve as witness to the miracle of light your act of courage brings to the world.

Sacred Sources for Inspiration and Insight

 anukkah celebrates not one miracle but two. There are the seven days that recall the intervention of God in unpredictable ways, the times, that is, when we did not give up (though we might have) and when a feeble initiative that ought to have died within a day lasted instead until we found a way to keep it going.

But the miracle of the first day is more awesome still. It is the unaccountable human penchant to light a flame in the first place, to dare to hope (against all odds) that if we can just get through at least one day, the defeat we fear just might not come....Light a candle in your soul and feel God's breath fan its flames until you find your own courage to go on.

Rabbi Lawrence Hoffman

 he command of God created day just as it created night, for every moment of the day and night has a purpose in God's plan. The recognition that God's ever present will is especially important at night, which represents the period of fear, failure, and exile.

Rabbi Samson Raphael Hirsch

e are the candle
lit by a spark from God.
Toward the heavens
our bright flame reaches
adding light to the world around us.
So fragile this flame. . . .

from Vataher Libenu, Congregation Beth El
of the Sudbury River Valley

eeding oil for eight days but having found oil that could last for only one, most people would not have lit the Temple candelabra at all. Why light when failure is certain? Why make the effort, if the effort is doomed? The miracle of the first day is that the Maccabees found the inner strength, the inner courage, to light the Menorah in the first place. They did not give up, for nothing is impossible, and in the end they prevailed.

No one is immune from feeling loneliness, from moments of darkness and night. But...light can remove darkness, day follows night. The message of Hanukkah is to kindle the first light: to care, to be concerned and to lift others. "In the end," the Hasidic masters said, "a little bit of light has the power to drive away the darkness."

Rabbi Avi Weiss

The Second Night, The Second Light
HODA'AH:
THE LIGHT OF GRATITUDE

Learning

osephus Flavius, the Jewish historian of the Hellenistic period who lived in the first century of the common era, wrote that Hanukkah is called the Festival of Lights because the deliverance of our people was "like a flash of lightning." *Nes Gadol Hayah Sham*—A Great Miracle Happened There. These words are inscribed on every dreidel outside of the land of Israel, proclaiming in a simple way that basic truth which is essential to our celebration of Hanukkah. But the miracle of light should not be consigned to the distant past, to a far off place, as the dreidel seems to suggest. Perhaps it would be better if all dreidels were to read *Nes Gadol Hayah Poh*—A Great Miracle Happened **Here**, as the dreidels of the land of Israel unabashedly announce. The Israeli dreidel brings its message—and us—closer to home, closer to our roots as Jews. That miracle is indeed our miracle. It repeats itself daily in our own lives, in everything that we do. And all we have to is look for its light.

Throughout the festival, we turn the dreidel. Perhaps it is the child within us that yearns to play. But much more than a innocent child's toy, the dreidel asserts our confidence in the world as God has given it to us. In the struggle against darkness, the forces of light won out. And we are free. It doesn't always seem that way in our history. Too often, the world seemed as if it was to be dark forever. Each time we spin the dreidel, the message is the same. We just don't always remember it. And as the dreidel spins out of control and proclaims its succinct message to a dizzy world, we are grateful that we are not the ones spinning. For the moment—for these eight days of celebration—we slow life down, reign it in, enough to gaze at the gentle light we have helped to bring into the world.

We express our thanks each day in the words of the Amidah prayer, adding a special paragraph these eight days of celebration. And as these words ease up from the soul in unbridled emotion, we bend the knee and bow the head in prayer in acknowledgement of the One who stands above—and beside us—throughout our lives, throughout our Maccabean struggles and those of everyday living.

And each day during these eight, we celebrate with the Hallel, psalms of praise, grateful for the chance to celebrate life. As we light the candles in the _hanukkiyah_, we are mindful of its message, grateful for its light.

Doing

as we celebrate Hanukkah each year, we kindle lights—one more each night—in order to teach one another and in so doing remind ourselves about the miraculous power inherent in God's light. We who are so aware of its resplendent glow want to express our gratitude for it by sharing that light—and its message—with others. As our tradition suggests, one must gaze into the flame, recall what it represents, and express gratitude for the triumph of Torah light over darkness.

And so we begin with a humble prayer of thanksgiving. It sounds easy. But as adults we are not always comfortable in doing things that once seemed to come so naturally to us as children. Sometimes we have to learn anew how to be grateful and express the sense of gratitude that may be hidden **deep** inside the recesses of our soul.

Here's one way to begin. Listen to the words of *Al Hanissim*: "We thank You for the miraculous deliverance, for the heroism, for the triumph in battle of our ancestors in other days and in our times." Let the words weave its melody of gratitude for you until you are ready to sing your own song, the one that emerges from your own experience of deliverance and thanksgiving. Repeat those words to yourself throughout the day. Let them become your mantra of Hanukkah and thanksgiving. Then go out and teach your song to others. Begin with your family, those you know and love. Tell them that you are grateful for their friendship and love. But don't be afraid to tell a stranger. That's the way we transform a stranger into a friend.

Sacred Sources for Inspiration and Insight

 arly in the morning on the 25th day of the ninth month, which is the month of Kislev...they rose and offered sacrifices as the Torah directs on the new altar of burnt offering which they had built. At the very season and on the very day the [Seleucids] had profaned it, it was dedicated with songs and harps and lutes and cymbals. All the people fell on their faces and worshiped, all in an effort to praise Heaven who had made them prosper. So they celebrated the dedication of the altar for eight days, and offered burnt offerings with gladness; they offered a sacrifice of deliverance and praise.

I Maccabees 4:52-56

A Thanksgiving Prayer

 ord, God of color!
God of yellow dawns and orange dusks,
Of plush green fields and cracked brown
    river beds,
Of blue skies and grey clouds.
God of rich, black earth and the white snow
    that covers it,
Of golden sunshine and clear, lucid raindrops.

Lord, God of Shapes!
God of pentagons and hexagons and squares,
Of elliptical orbits and triangular cones,
Of perfect circles and imperfect spheres.
God of trapezoids and rectangles and straight
    lines and curves.

Lord, God of sizes!
God of giant sequoias and tiny bacteria,
Of bottomless caverns and lofty mountain peaks,
Of mustard seeds and acorns and spores.
God of heights and depth and breadth.

Lord, God of creation!
God of everything that inhabits the earth,
And the earth itself!
Thank You for all Your creation with its endless variety,
And for our senses with which we perceive the myriad of
    creation.

Rabbi Roy Walters

The Third Night, The Third Light
TZEDAKAH:
THE LIGHT OF SHARING

Learning

e all think about gift-giving when talking about Hanukkah. Waiting in anticipation of Hanukkah fun, we've even created our own customs when it comes to gifts. In some families, the custom is one gift each night. For other families, each night has a different theme for the giving of gifts. In still other families, different nights are devoted to exchanging gifts with particular relatives: "Tonight is Uncle Lee and Aunt Jayne's night!" Maybe it is our way of competing with Christmas or maybe it is just our way of growing Hanukkah to its fullest.

The custom of giving gifts at Hanukkah may be more of a reflection of North American culture than it is of historical Jewish tradition. Perhaps it grew out of the comfort of the middle class, out of a generation which grew up with very little and grew accustom to much more. The idea of Hanukkah gelt (Yiddish for money), the core Hanukkah gift, for example, may have originally derived from a practice in seventeenth century Poland when children were given coins who, in turn, gave these coins (gelt) to their poorly paid teachers as a bonus. The time of the year for financial recognition, however modest, seemed logical since there

27

is indeed some connection between the root word for Hanukkah and the Hebrew word for education (hinukh). As communities became more affluent, parents gave children Hanukkah gelt to keep for themselves and to share with others, especially by encouraging them to drop a few of these coins in *pushkes* (charity boxes) that are found in many Jewish homes. Over time, the giving of coins was replaced by the giving of gifts. Somewhere along the way, when gifts replaced coins, it seems that we forgot about the sharing of these gifts with others.

Maybe we should look at Jewish communities throughout the world, what form the giving of gifts took in those places, and bring their lessons of life into our own. Indeed, I am certain that there may be something they can teach us. For example, when Syria boasted of a larger Jewish community, it was common for children to receive as a gift a *hamsa*-shaped candle to be used for Hanukkah. The *hamsa*—from the Arabic word for five—is a hand-shaped amulet used to ward off the evil eye, the *ayin ha-rah,* or as my bobbe used to say in one breath, "the *k'ayin ha-rah.*" And in Turkey, it is still common for families to share sweets with one another during the eight day Hanukkah week. Whatever the community, one thing was clear: Giving to others was inseparable from the celebration of Hanukkah.

Some people say that Hanukkah is a "minor festival" in the cycle of Jewish holidays and festivals. While that may be technically true, we know that there is much reason for us to celebrate. As the sheheheyanu prayer proclaims on the first night, "Thank you God for guiding us into this season, to this very point in time." We don't have to look far to realize that there are many in this world who barely survive—and many who just don't. Thank God, we have so much to share!

Doing

ach night during Hanukkah, we receive gifts. It's a lot of fun to give gifts and to receive them. No argument there. However, this evening, we are going to thank God for what we have in a special way, long accepted by the Jewish community as *the Jewish way*: by sharing it with others. Tonight, after the lighting of the candles and the singing of songs, we will accept no gifts for ourselves. Instead, we will leave the comforts of our home behind and give gifts to those less fortunate than we are. In doing so, the gift we receive this Hanukkah night will be found in the giving of ourselves to someone else. It's *tzedakah* logic: the more we give away, the more we gain.

There are lots of things to do. Here is a list to get you started, but don't let your imagination end here:

1. Volunteer at a local "feeding the homeless" program. Bring the food with you. Remember to call ahead to make arrangements.

2. Collect canned goods for a local food pantry. Get your neighborhood friends involved. When you invite your friends to a Hanukkah party and they ask "what can I bring?" tell them to bring some canned goods. Then distribute them together.

3. Participate in a "toys for tots" collection program. Don't restrict your tzedakah to the Jewish community. There is often enough time between Hanukkah and Christmas for this to be a good interchange between faith communities.

4. Especially in northern climates, winter is a rough time for the poor and homeless. Collect hats, gloves, scarfs and winter clothing and distribute to people who make their homes on the streets or in temporary shelters.

Sacred Sources for Inspiration and Insight

 A Rebbe's Proverb (From the Yiddish)

f you always assume

the man sitting next to you

is the Messiah

waiting for some simple kindness—

You will soon come to weigh your words

and watch your hands.

And if he so chooses

not to reveal himself

in your time—

It will not matter.

Danny Siegel, *And God Braided Eve's Hair*

believe that giving and receiving are two sides of the same currency that circulates with a constantly changing balance at all times, among the ever succeeding generations of Jewish philanthropists great and small. Giving and receiving are relational, like up and down; they could not exist without each other, and they interpenetrate each other's realm. I would even go so far as to speculate that great acts of *tzedakah* themselves, or instances, in times of crisis, of great self-sacrifice—do not exist in a pure form. Most parents I know would if, God forbid, they had to, give their own lives so that their children might live. And yet in those last moments before this horrible sentence were carried out, might there not also come an exquisite self-knowledge and fulfillment that perhaps might be worth all the paler satisfactions of many unlived years.... [*Tzedakah*] is in the design of human nature. And to cast giving as the opposite of receiving—as in the conventional wisdom that "it's better to give than to receive"—is to miss the point of *tzedakah* entirely.

Allan Appel

The Fourth Night, The Fourth Light
TORAH:
THE LIGHT OF KNOWLEDGE

Learning

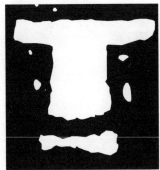

orah gives of its own light—and keeps on giving infinitely. By sharing its brilliance with others, the light of Torah is increased rather than diminished, as one might typically expect of something. That's part of its unique nature. Some of our teachers have suggested that Torah is written with black fire on white fire. Thus, those who study Torah are illuminated by the fiery radiance of its message. Remember when Moses came down the mountain called Sinai? He was changed by his journey up Sinai, transformed. The Torah text suggests that the people surrounding the foot of the mountain could actually see the change in his eyes. They sparkled with the splendor of Torah.

As we enter the lives of our ancestors through the pages of sacred text, we actually become them. As we study, the lives of our ancestors become intertwined with our own. Their struggles become our struggles. Like us, they face the daily challenges of faith which the world forces on us. And when we leave the text—only to return at some later time—these Biblical ancestors have left a bit of themselves in us and we have left a part of ourselves in the sacred text. Through our encounter with the text, we have joined our own story with the history of our people.

33

Thus, whether it was Judah whom the people called Maccabee (the Hammer), Hannah and her seven sons, or the mysterious Judith, we have entered their struggle for freedom—and become part of it. And we are obligated to continue that struggle by celebrating it and extending it, bringing it forward for the next generation. As contemporary songwriter Doug Cotler's verse has it: "We are freedom's inheritance." It is our obligation as Jews. None of us are truly free until we are all free. And the study of Torah helps us to understand the depth of that freedom.

Doing

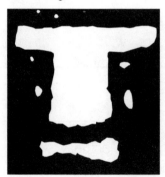
onight we study—as you should every day. (This evening, wait until the lights have finished burning.) Hanukkah is the only time of year when Torah is publicly read (each morning) for eight days in a row. Study is more than just a routine reading of the text. The Torah is God's love letter to the Jewish people. Caress its edges. Ponder each word. Breathe in its mystical fragrance. Our study brings us closer to God and, as a result, closer to our essential selves. That's the awesome power of Torah study. That's what Judah and his brothers sought to protect.

According to Jewish mystical tradition, when one studies simply for the sake of study, what the tradition calls *Torah lishma*, that person causes the Shekhinah, God's indwelling presence, to be united with the *Kadosh Barukh Hu*, the Holy Blessed One. Thus, according to the mystics, the redemption of the world depends on our study. Maybe that's what the rabbis had in mind when they taught that "Talmud Torah (study) is more important than other *mitzvot*" because it leads us to them all.

So, tonight, get out a sacred text and start studying. Find yourself a "study buddy" and study with a friend; you tend to see much more in the text that way. Teach one another and allow the text to instruct you both. The Zohar teaches, "In each word shines many lights." Words of Torah actually can illumine our path in the world.

Sacred Sources for Inspiration and Insight

et your fine oil pour through
the eight branches of the menorah
and your goodness flow
toward every living thing,
so that all may drink
from the river of light.

For you are the Keeper
of the fountain of life;
and in your light
do we see light.

Rabbi Yaakov Bar Nachman,
based on a kabbalistic meditation
by Rabbi Moses Albaz

erhaps a meditation is a daydream, a daydream of the soul as the beloved and God, the lover, their meeting in the tryst of prayer, their yearning for one another after parting; a daydream of their being untied again.

Or perhaps a meditation is the becoming aware of the human soul of its loneliness and the anticipation of its being united with the One who transcends the All and is able to come past one's own defenses.

Or perhaps, again, it is a standing back with the whole of the cosmos before one's mind's eye as one's heart is being filled with the sheer joy of seeing the balance of the All and one's own self as part of it.

Or perhaps a searching into one's own motives, values, and wishes, with the light of the Torah against the background of the past.

Or perhaps . . .

Rabbi Zalman Schacter-Shalomi

The Fifth Night, The Fifth Light
AVODAH:
THE LIGHT OF SERVICE

Learning

have always had a sense that throughout the three year battle, Judah the Maccabee understood that he and his brothers were not fighting alone. Judah was more than just a courageous young man forced by circumstance to become a soldier. And it was not merely his brilliance as a military strategist which brought victory that the people celebrated. Judah understood that he was not the lone source of his strength. His faith in God propelled him to prevail over his enemy. It may have taken centuries for our people to fully comprehend the depth of his faith—and even forgotten about it during the reign of some of his descendants—but we have done so.

Philosopher/theologian Rabbi Eugene Borowitz teaches that Judaism is an ideal which all Jews must endeavor to reach. By doing God's work in the world, we can stand strong against the tide. This was Judah's cause. Let's make it our own, as well.

As the psalmist has poignantly penned, "The voice of Adonai kindles flames of fire" (Psalm 29:7). Think about that for a moment. The medieval Jewish mystic Abraham Abulafia was correct when he wrote, "the voice of God can be found within the flame—and it also dwells within the heart." Judah's heart was on

37

fire as he passionately pursued his mission. It is that sense of passion that Hanukkah can help us recapture in our own lives.

The power of Hanukkah and its celebration has captivated Jews throughout our history whether in times of persecution or in freedom. Hundreds of stories came with the survivors of the Holocaust about how Hanukkah was celebrated "in those days, at this season," bringing a bit of light into those dark years and dark places.

One story comes from the Bergen-Belsen concentration camp in Germany near Hanover. The Nazi guards knew when Hanukkah arrived and offered a bit of margarine as a gift to the group's rabbi. When the rabbi reached out to accept the gift, the guard dropped it to the floor and ordered the rabbi to lick up the margarine. Unbeknownst to those who witnessed the event, as the rabbi was on the floor, he carefully scraped some of the margarine into his pocket. After the guards left, the rabbi announced to his followers, "We have oil." He removed some threads from his jacket for a wick. Others joined him in creating a makeshift menorah. One person had an extra spoon, a second added a button, and a third provided an empty can. Though fragile, this menorah shined its light into the next world. Those who witnessed the event remember its glow. These Jews served God by bringing light into the world.

Doing

To be in God's service is do God's work in the world, to take the light that has been given to us and kindle the lamp of others. We are the channel through which God's blessings flow into the world. We are partners in the ongoing work of creation. According to Rabbi Joseph Soloveitchik, the will of the Maccabees to fulfill the *mitzvah* of lighting the menorah in the ancient Temple propelled them to begin what appeared to be a hopeless search for oil among the Temple debris. They succeeded. It seems that this desire to battle all odds for the sake of bringing God's light to the world represents the miracle of Jewish survival.

Rabbi Bernard Raskas tells the story about a young man who was apprenticed to a blacksmith learned how to hold the tongs, lift the hammer, strike the anvil and blow the fire with the bellows. After completing his apprenticeship, he was employed by the royal smithy. But the young man's delight at his appointment soon turned to despair when he discovered that he had failed to learn how to kindle a spark.

Have you ever thought about the *shammash* candle? Without the spark, without that first light, there can be no more. Ḥanukkah is more than lighting candles, spinning dreidels, and eating greasy foods fried in oil. It is about nurturing that spark, the one that glows inside each of us, until it bursts into flame.

The author of the book of Proverbs understood this idea. She knew that *mitzvot* bring us closer to God. Listen to her words:

"For the mitzvah is a lamp, and the teaching is a light" (Proverbs 6:23).

Sometimes we do God's work by simply allowing God's message to flow through us, through what we do into the world. Things don't always happen that way. Therefore, often we must look to our tradition and its system of *mitzvot* (divine instructions) for guidance. From a distant place in our past, we hear the call echoing through history, "Be thou a blessing."

Decide how you are going to keep that spark lit. Perhaps by lending some money to someone who needs to start a business or keep her family going during the dark days of winter. Maybe you want to send an anonymous check to that relative who you know needs helps but is too proud to ask for it. Or help an elderly neighbor fix a roof or a leaky faucet. Or support an organization that promotes or defends religious or political freedom. Or, for the sake of *klal Yisrael* (the entire Jewish community and its survival), especially important to remember when we consider the way the Maccabean wars split the Jewish community, reach out to members of a Jewish community who represent a different approach to Judaism than you do. Whatever you decide to do, just remember: there are lots of ways to repair a broken world.

Sacred Sources for Inspiration and Insight

 ask only one thing of God.

A solitary thing do I seek:

That I may stay close to God all the days of my life,

and in this Divine light,

[be given the privilege just] to think about God's presence.

Psalm 27:4

 As roots seek the source of their sustenance

As branches soar toward the life-giving light

So do we, rooted in blessing,

Reach upward in faith and deed

To become a blessing.

Dolores Wilkenfeld

 he 16th century Kabbalist, Isaac Luria Ashkenazi (the ARI) detailed the intricate process of creation. He explained that when God decided to create the world there was no space in which to do so because God was occupying all the space and time that existed. God therefore contracted within God's Self to make room for the world. God filled the newly emptied space with the heavens and the earth.

41

However, as a consequence of this retraction, none of God's presence was in the world. God therefore breathed a little light back into the world, just as one might exhale after inhaling. Special vessels were created to hold God's powerful light. These vessels trapped and radiated the divine effulgence until, mysteriously, they could no longer hold the light. Suddenly, the vessels burst apart, filling the world with a chaotic dance of broken shards and sparks of light.

The Jew's task is to identify and—through *mitzvot*—to recover the divine sparks in the world, thereby restoring wholeness to creation. In short, the world is broken and we are to be its. "fixers."

Rabbi Nancy Flam, The Outstretched Arm

The Sixth Night, The Sixth Light
BINAH:
THE LIGHT OF UNDERSTANDING

Learning

ach year, as we see the glow of light from the Hanukkah candles—or burning oil if you like a more "authentic" burn—reflected in faces of our family, we come to an understanding about growing. As our children grow into maturity, we realize that we too are growing—growing older. These are special moments that we remember, even as others fade into the deep recesses of memory. These memories become part of the legacy of our people, ones that we pass through the generations, heaped on top of those we ourselves inherited. We may not be able to recreate the experience of our distant ancestors or even our most familiar grandparents—and we shouldn't even try—but we can do our best to claim the experience as our own. Through the process, we become sacred texts.

Binah, understanding, is a gift of time. One doesn't just get it overnight. One grows into it. So tonight, we celebrate the understanding that comes through growth. We think about the past, the travels of our people, the journey of our ancestors, where life has taken us. And we marvel at our ability to make sense out of this complex world.

Rabbi Micha Odenheimer teaches us that according to Rabbi Pinchas of Koretz, the Hanukkah candles cast forth light from the infinite, hidden storehouse of primordial illumination. This light has the power to make our dreams transparent, so that we can see the radiance of God through them. I guess we never realized that the light was so strong.

Doing

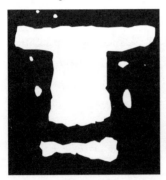

onight we take the time for ourselves and our children. That's right. No work tonight—even though Hanukkah allows it (after the candles burn completely down). No T.V. or rushing out to the movies or theater. Just us. Family and friends, talking, playing, enjoying the simple company of one another.

And if you are alone—with family far away—pick up the telephone. Better yet, make a new friend. Invite him to share the light of Hanukkah with you. Chances are she's lonely too.

There is a tradition that suggests that God hasn't stopped speaking to us since beginning the dialogue on Mt. Sinai. We heard the message then, because the desert was awash with silence. We have difficulty hearing the message today, because there is just too much "noise" in the world. Tonight, we have the opportunity to quiet the noise and listen. Just listen.

Abraham Joshua Heschel taught us that the challenge of modern living is to make time holy. It is perhaps our most important Jewish gift to the world. Here's your chance to transform time by making it holy.

Sacred Sources for Inspiration and Insight

he kids' faces, slightly saffron-colored in the candlelight, change so much from year to year. They grow older so quickly. The babyhood delight at anything new changes to childlike anticipation of wonderful treats, which in turn, gives way to mixed pre-adolescent messages of forthright greed and subdued wonder at the meaning beyond the presents.... The Israeli dreidel is right: Hanukkah's great miracle happened in Israel. But as our children gather in the candle glow, I think we too could spin an Israeli dreidel, for a great miracle happens here, as well, in every home where the candles' flame illuminate the path from the past the way to the future.

Erica Meyer Rauzin

Hannah's Prayer over her slain children

y children, O my children. I do not know how you entered my "kishkes." I did not fashion you in my womb, nor did I bequeath life and soul to you. I did not raise or exult you. Rather, Adonai, the God of Israel, created you. God built up your frame, wove your veins, grew flesh over you, covered it with skin, sprouted hair over it, breathed the life into you, and brought you out into the light of this world and its air. Now since you chose to give up your lives for God's holy Torah, to die a quick death and to depart from a short life, God will return your souls to you, will return breath to you and you will live. You will be saved from eternal death and will inherit the eternal life, my children, and God will reward you for your deeds. You are fortunate, and fortunate are your parents! May God's providence be with you as God was with those who came before you.

2 Maccabees 7

he old will be rejuvenated, the new will be consecrated; old and new together will be torches of light over Zion.

Rabbi Abraham Isaac Kook

The Seventh Night, The Seventh Light
AHAVAH:
THE LIGHT OF LOVE

Learning

n some Sefardic communities, Hanukkah's seventh night—and seventh light—is dedicated to Jewish women for their bravery during the Maccabean war. They refused to be humiliated by the enemy. They refused to be victims even when it cost them their lives. Since it is one of the few times historically in which women are given unconditional acknowledgement (It's about time!), such acts of heroism are particularly worthy of memory. This recognition of women may also reflect the influence on Hanukkah of the unusual and little known tale from the Apocrypha (those books which didn't quite make it into the Hebrew Bible) of Judith who cut off the head (yuk!) of Holofernes, a Greek general—and saved the Jewish people—as he slept off his drunken stupor. According to the account of the story, when Holofernes' soldiers saw what had happened to their ferocious leader, they were frightened and fled Jerusalem, allowing Judah and the Maccabees to cleanse the Temple and restore it.

North African Jewish women and girls fill the synagogue at Hanukkah. Even in those traditional synagogues where women may not approach the Torah (this is not the time nor place for that debate!), they are given the honor of removing the Torah scrolls and kissing them. For their acts of heroism during the Maccabean Wars, they have become our Torah scrolls. My female friends, this is your chance: Be Torah.

In this generation, we have finally realized all of the things that women have taught us—and have yet to teach us. As a result, our lifestyles have changed. Women have taught us, in particular, that love is the force that holds this fragile world together. They have shown us all how to express love without embarrassment, without shame, and extend this love to all.

Hanukkah killjoys like to remind us that Hanukkah is technically a minor festival. Call it what you like, Hanukkah has major Torah to teach us. Look at what Rabbi Lawrence Hoffman has to say about the power of Hanukkah and its influence on our lives: "How difficult it is to start again, to reawaken love lying dormant, or dream again of purpose when youthful idealism has been unfairly jaded: when marriages turn out to require daytime work as much as nighttime romance; when we learn what it is like to be fired, not just hired; when daily routine so hardens us that we forget how to smell the flowers or hope for the sun; when the Hanukkah-like flame of our own inner dedication is dampened in ways no one is prepared us for, and when we begin to suspect that it is too late to set the world on fire again."

When we see the lights of the *hanukkiyah*, when we smell the latkes frying in the pan, when we see the dreidel spinning wildly in a miraculous frenzy, we know that the light of Divine love still burns deeply within our soul. And we know that even when we may be experiencing personal pain, we can yet love again.

Doing

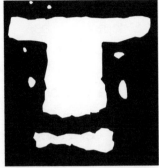

oo many among us have forgotten how to express love in the modern world. We may not even know what the word represents any longer. It has found its way into so many other places that we may have lost hold of its meaning. To make matters worse, we are bombarded by media messages that mislead us, seduced into believing love is something else when it is not. Love ain't sex; don't deceive yourself into thinking that that's all there is to it. And love isn't perfect either. Not when it's human. Love is the coming together of two human beings in their struggle of everyday living. Love is the means through which we bring *shalom*, tranquility, into the world and into our life. Love is the dream on which reality is built. You can find it, but only if you are willing to give some of it away.

Go ahead, spread your love in the world. And begin with your loving self.

In recognition of this seventh night, let's work for equality for women in the Jewish world. More than just tolerance, let us embrace equality as a goal for all people. As an expression of your love for others, do something about it. Start with your own family, your own synagogue, your own community. Make sure that women—all people, as a matter of fact—have an equal role in every part of society which is yours.

Sacred Sources for Inspiration and Insight

ne Passover, my daughter came home from college and shared the results of a dorm "bull session." Trying to figure out why she hadn't turned to drinking, drugs or carefree sex as had a number of those with whom she grew up, she had only one answer, "Hanukkah." Her reasoning, "When we had to celebrate Hanukkah while everyone else celebrated Christmas, I learned that it was O.K. to be different. I didn't have to do everything that everyone else did."

Patti Goldin
adapted from *Building Jewish Life*: Hanukkah

lessed is the match consumed in kindling flame.

Blessed is the flame that burns in the heart's secret places.

Blessed is the heart with strength to stop its beating for honor's sake.

Blessed is the match consumed in kindling flame.

Hannah Senesh

The Eighth Night, The Eighth Light
TIKVAH:
LIGHT OF HOPE

Learning

anukkah is usually translated as dedication or *rededication*, referring to the ancient Temple in Jerusalem which had been defiled by Antiochus in his attempt to Hellenize Judea. One of the acts of rededication was the lighting of the Temple's seven-branched menorah which was kept perpetually burning as a reminder of God's presence in our midst. This ancient symbol predates the magen david (star of David) considerably. The light of the menorah reminds us that we are not alone in the world—although it sometimes seems that way. There is a world of meaning far beyond what our eyes see. It is the spark in our soul which lights our way into that world.

In a sense, Hanukkah is only part of the whole realm of rededication in Judaism. We spend our whole lives working at holiness until the final redemption comes. That's when the process of rededication, of Hanukkah, is completed. According to mystical tradition, when the Hanukkah lights are kindled, the or *ganuz*, the messianic light that has been hidden away since Creation, is revealed in the radiance of its tapers.

Even during the darkest days of our history—and there were plenty of them—our people lived with hope. Too often, that's all they had. We dreamed of a better world and prayed for the opportunity to makes those dreams real. Perhaps it is one of the many things that kept alive during those periods of darkness. That sense of hope is our legacy as Jews. It is what we have to offer to the world. Louis Brandeis once said that what makes the Jewish people unique is not that they dream, for all peoples do, but that history has given us the strength and the courage to realize our dreams.

As the Hanukkah candles burn for the last time this year, struggling against the darkness of the night, let the flames not smolder and die. Instead, let the memory of their light drive you forward, committed to make your dreams real. It is never too late, never! According to the tradition of the kabbalists, we have until the very end of Hanukkah to finish the work of *teshuvah*, of turning, that we started before Yom Kippur. It's one of the reasons why the rabbis refer to this last day of Hanukkah as *Zot* Hanukkah—*this* is Hanukkah. This indeed is the essence of its celebration.

The act of lighting candles each night during Hanukah is only temporal. It is bound by the eight days of celebration. The gentle lights of the *hanukkiyah* shine their unyielding beacon of hope from time into eternity. The lights shine with their message of hope, because they are part of the light which will come with ultimate redemption. Yet, the challenge that confronts us this night and every night during the year is how we do our part in extending this redemptive light into the world.

Doing

ach day during Hanukkah, and every day during the year, we march against the darkness, praying that it will be followed by light. Hours later, our fears are laid to rest when light creeps into the world until the entire world is ablaze with God's radiant light. Even in the bleakest days of winter, God rolls away the darkness to make room for the light. Rabbi A. Alan Steinbach said it best when he wrote, "Out of the shadows of night, the world rolls into light. It is daybreak everywhere." But we need not wait for the light. We can force the light of day into the dark crevices of the world by what we do with our lives and how we make them holy.

Some people use Hanukkah as an opportunity to make a *mizrah* plaque and place it on the eastern wall of one's home to remind us of the direction of Jerusalem—the site of the Hanukkah miracle. It is a good way to help center our lives.

This night, after the candles have concluded their own journey of light, begin yours. Consider what you will do to bring the needed change in your own life, in your own way of living. Write down your plans. Make sure they are written on your heart. Discuss them with family and friends. Often the support of those whom we love—and who love us—make the changes a lot easier. Then make the preparations required for your journey.

Sacred Sources for Inspiration and Insight

hen came the eighth day, when the whole row burns, even the faithful ninth, the servant sham-mash, which on other nights is used only for the lighting of the others. A great slendour streamed from the Menorah. The children's eyes glistened. But for our friend all this was the symbol of the enkindling of a nation. When there is but one light all is still dark, and the solitary light looks melancholy. Soon it finds one companion, then another and another. The darkness must retreat. The light comes first to the young and the poor—then others join who love Justice, Truth, Liberty, Progress, Humanity, and Beauty. When all the candles burn, then we must all stand and rejoice over the achievement. And no office can be more blessed than that of a Servant of the Light.

from "The Menorah," by Theodor Herzl
translated by B. L. Pouzzner

he first time that Adam saw the sun go down and an ever deepening gloom enfold creation, his mind was filled with terror. Then God took pity on him, and endowed him with the divine intuition to take two stones—the name of one was Darkness and the name of the other was the Shadow of Death—and rub them against each other, and to discover fire. Suddenly, Adam exclaimed with grateful joy: "Praised be the Creator of Light!"

Babylonian Talmud, Avodah Zarah 8b

DREIDELS, LATKES AND EVERYTHING ELSE

Playing Dreidel:

The dreidel probably evolved from a German gambling game. While Jewish tradition generally discourages gambling as a form of robbery (since you didn't work for the profit), the dreidel game is one of the few instances of holiday celebration that tolerates any form of gambling. The dreidel game was designed to emphasize the miracle of Hanukkah. Thus, each side of the dreidel is inscribed with a Hebrew letter Nun, Gimmel, Heh, Shin for: **N**es **G**adol **H**ayah **S**ham.

Taking turns, one person spins the dreidel at a time. Whether one wins or loses is determined by which side of the dreidel faces up when it falls.

a.   *Nun* stands for nothing (nisht in Yiddish) so the player does nothing.
b.   *Gimmel* stands for all (gantz in Yiddish) so the player takes everything in the pot.
c.   *Heh* stands for half (halb in Yiddish) so the player takes half of what is in the pot.
d.   *Shin* stands for put in (shtel in Yiddish) so the player puts one in the pot.

Potato Latkes

ingredients:

   3 large potatoes (2 cups grated)
   1 small onion
   2 eggs (egg whites for the cholesterol conscious)
   2 tablespoons flour or matzah meal (if you have some left over)
   1 teaspoon salt

Grate potatoes and place them in a bowl. Grate in the onion. Add eggs, flour, and salt. Drain off excess liquid. Drop by spoonfuls into well-oiled frying pan. Fry on both sides in hot oil. Serve with apple sauce or sour cream.

No Peel Latkes

ingredients:

>1 egg
>
>1 small onion cut into quarters
>
>3 cups of unpeeled potatoes, cut into cubes
>
>2 tablespoons flour
>
>1 tablespoon oil
>
>1/4 teaspoon sugar
>
>1/2 teaspoon salt
>
>1/8 teaspoon pepper

Blend the egg and onion for a few seconds in a blender. Add half the potatoes. Blend until smooth. Add the other ingredients. Blend until smooth. Drop by spoonfuls into a well-oiled frying pan. Fry on both sides. Drain on a paper towel. Serve with apple sauce or sour cream.

Light Latkes

ingredients:

>3 large potatoes, peeled and grated
>
>1/4 cup grated onion
>
>1/4 cup egg substitute (or egg whites only)
>
>1/2 teaspoon salt
>
>1/4 teaspoon baking powder
>
>3 tablespoons matzah meal

Place grated potatoes in ice water for an hour. Drain well and press out excess moisture. Place in mixing bowl and add onion and egg sub substitute and mix well. In a small bowl, combine salt, baking powder and matzah meal. Slowly add to potato mixture, mixing very well. Drop by tablespoon onto hot, lightly oiled or sprayed skillet. Cook on one side until well-browned, turn over and brown other side.

Naomi Arbit

Sufganiot (known as bunuellos among Spanish Jews)

ingredients:

3/4 cup orange juice or water
1/4 lb. margarine
4 tablespoons sugar
2 packages dry yeast
3 cups flour
2 eggs, beaten
1 dash of salt

Combine orange juice, margarine and sugar and heat until margarine melts. Cool to lukewarm and add yeast. Stir until dissolved. Combine all ingredients and mix. Knead until smooth. (You may need to add more flour.) Place dough in greased bowl and cover. Let rise in a warm spot for a half hour. Punch down. Shape small pieces of dough into balls, rings, or twists. Cover and let rise another half hour. Deep fry in hot oil. Drain. Put a few teaspoons of powered sugar or cinnamon in a paper bag. Add doughnuts and shake.

Labtah

Ingredients:

6 tablespoons oil
2 lbs. cooked potatoes
4 eggs
4 oz. walnuts, chopped
2 teaspoons salt
1/4 teaspoon white pepper

to garnish:

walnuts
chopped lettuce

Heat the oil in a heavy pan. Mash the potatoes, eggs, copped walnuts, salt and pepper. Fry into one large (traditional pattern) or 8 small pancakes until crusted and golden on both sides. Garnish with walnuts and chopped lettuce. Serve hot. Serves 8.

Jewish Cooking for Pleasure

GLOSSARY

Antiochus IV Epiphanes: Syrian king (175 - 163 BCE) who plundered the Temple. He forbade the Jews to observe their religious practices and forcefully tried to Hellenize Judea. These actions led to the uprising of the Maccabees

atayif: pancake filled with nuts and honey, popular among Sefardic Jews

bunellos: raised doughnuts, often shaped light ropes of dough, popular among Spanish Jews

dreidel: (Hebrew, sevivon) spinning top used in Hanukkah games, inscribed with four Hebrew letters: nun, gimel, heh, shin/peh

fritelle di Hanukkah: raisin-flecked diamonds of dough that have been fried in olive oil, then dipped in honey, eaten by Italian Jews

gelt: candy given in the form of money for Hanukkah, may be traced to an idea which emphasizes the sweetness of Torah study

Hannah: mother who, along with her seven sons, were slain for refusing to bow to an idol

hanukkiyah: candle holder specifically used for Hanukkah, may hold oil, as well

Hasidim: religious purists (opponents of the Hellenizers), not to be confused with contemporary *Hasidim,* recognized by their *payot* (earlocks), fur hats and long black coats

Hasmonean: the family name of the dynasty founded by Mattathias

labtah: pancakes of mashed potatoes and nuts, eaten by European Georgian Jews

loukomades: deep-fried puffs of dough, eaten by Greek Jews

latke/s: potato pancake/s (Hebrew, *levivah/levivot*)

Maccabees: rebel army who fought the Syrian-Greeks in 165 B.C.E.

Mattathias: father of the five Hasmonean brothers who initiated and led the revolt against the Syrian-Greeks; he was succeeded by his third son Judah

menorah: candle holder (in modern Hebrew, light bulb)

ner: candle, light

Nes Gadol Hayah Poh/Sham: A Great Miracle Happened Here/There—inscribed on the dreidel *persumat hanes:* literally, to make known the miracle

shammash (shammos): often called "servant candle," use this candle to light other candles

shemen: oil

shemen zayit: olive oil

sufganiah/sufganiot: jelly doughnut/s, popular among Israelis, called pontichikes by some Ashkenazic Jews

zelabi: snail-shaped, fried pastries eaten by Persian Jews

Zot Hanukkah: literally, "this is Hanukkah," refers to the last day of Hanukkah, taken from designated Torah reading, reflects a notion that "this is the essence of Hanukkah"

SOURCES FOR FURTHER REFLECTION

Meditation prior to lighting candles

May it be your will, Adonai, my God and God of my ancestors, that this be a favorable time before You to fulfill the *mitzvah* of lighting the Hanukkah lamp, as if I had fathomed all of the awesome secrets sealed in it. May it ascend before You with the intent of this *mitzvah* as it is performed by Your beloved children, who concentrate on all Your sacred Names that are recalled by this lighting, who elevate the unification and pairing of the holy, supreme Attributes, and illuminate the Great Luminaries through Your powerful Presence [the Shekhinah]. From there, may an emanation be directed to me, Your servant (*Hebrew name*) son/daughter of (*parents' names*) to illuminate through them the Lights of Life. "For it is You who will light my lamp, Adonai, my God, who will illuminate my darkness."

adapted from *Siddur Otzar HaTefillot*

A kavannah, prior to lighting the candles

May these trembling flames
The flames of our soul
And the warm glow kindled this night
By the children of Israel
Fuse, Fuse, Fuse in the light of Your presence.

from *Vataher Libenu*, Congregation Beth El
of the Sudbury River Valley

Psalm 30. *(traditionally read by Sefardim after the lighting of the candles, called the Song of the Day in the mishnah)*

A psalm of David,
A song for the [re]dedication of the Temple.

I celebrate You, Adonai,
    for it if You who has lifted me up.
    and not let my adversaries triumph over me.
Adonai, my God,
    I cried out to You,
    and You healed me.
You brought me up from Sheol,
    preserved me from going down into the pits.
You who are faithful to God, sing to God,
    praise God's well-deserved reputation.
For God is angry only momentarily
    there is life when God is pleased
    Weeping may delay the [end of the] night,
    but at dawn there are shouts of joy.

When I was free of trouble,
    I thought that nothing could shake me up
    for when You, Adonai, were pleased [with me],
    You made me as sturdy as a mighty mountain.

When You hid your face
    I was panic-stricken.
I called out to You, Adonai,
    to my God I appealed.
"What is to be gained from my death,
    were I to descend into the Pit?"
Could I as dust praise You?
Would I be able to declare my faith in You?
Hear me now, Adonai; have mercy on me;
    Adonai, help me!"

61

You turned my lament into dancing,

you unfastened my sackcloth and clothed me with joy,

so that I could sing endless praises to You with my entire being;

Adonai, my God, I will praise You forever.

Maoz Tzur

(traditionally sung by Ashkenzim after the lighting of the candles)

מָעוֹז צוּר יְשׁוּעָתִי

לְךָ נָאֶה לְשַׁבֵּחַ

תִּכּוֹן בֵּית תְּפִלָּתִי

וְשָׁם תּוֹדָה נְזַבֵּחַ.

לְעֵת תָּכִין מַטְבֵּחַ

מִצָּר הַמְנַבֵּחַ.

אָז אֶגְמוֹר בְּשִׁיר מִזְמוֹר

חֲנֻכַּת הַמִּזְבֵּחַ.

Rock of ages, let our song
Praise Your saving power.
You, amid the raging foes,
Were our sheltering tower
Furious, they assailed us,
But Your arm availed us,
And Your word
Broke their sword
When our own strength failed us.

Rock of All My Dreams

An alternative interpretation of Maoz Tzur

Rock of all my dreams
I'm anchored in your air
by my heart waking to you
in the house of the world
where these words like answered prayer
as real as conversation:
You built that justice

and the deeper landscape
in which I may walk away
from ruin and despair
and those who would kill me—
rising in all my pasts
to annihilate us—
and into new life
where we imagine a day of completing
a place for you again
in the words we find like new bricks
still warm from the heart's altar—
these words so glad to be at home
they build you a rededication
to match the psalms of Hanukkah.

David Rosenberg, *A Blazing Fountain*

Psalm 67 *(Jewish tradition maintains that this psalm was revealed to Moses and David in the form of a seven-branched menorah on a golden tablet with the words etched on the branches and stem.)*

For the leader, with instrumental music.
A psalm, a song.

May God be gracious to us and bless us.
    May God show us favor. Selah.
so that Your way can be known [throughout] the earth,
    Your deliverance among all nations.

People will praise You, O God;
    all peoples will praise You.
Nations will revel and shout for joy,
    for You guide all people equally,
    advising the nations of the earth. Selah.
The peoples will praise You, O God;
    all peoples will praise You.

May the earth yield its produce;
    may God, *our God*, bless us.
May God bless us,
    and be revered
    from one end of the earth to the other.